THE STORY OF OLIVIA RODRIGO

An Inspiring Biography for Young Readers

— Written by —
Stacia Deutsch

— Illustrations by —
María Perera

callisto publishing
an imprint of Sourcebooks

To Temecula, California:
Olivia's hometown and mine, too!

Illustrations by María Perera with the following exception:
© Semicircular/Creative Market (map)
Author photo courtesy of Melissa Jacobs
Series Designer: Angela Navarra
Art Director: Angela Navarra
Art Producer: Stacey Stambaugh
Editor: Kristen Depken
Production Editor: Rachel Taenzler
Production Designer: Martin Worthington

Published by Callisto Publishing LLC C/O Sourcebooks LLC
P.O. Box 4410, Naperville, Illinois 60567-4410
(630) 961-3900
callistopublishing.com

Library of Congress Cataloging-in-Publication Data is on file with the publisher.

This product conforms to all applicable CPSC and CPSIA standards.

Source of Production: Versa Press
Date of Production: December 2025
Run Number: 5061843

Printed and bound in the United States of America.

VP 10 9 8 7 6 5 4 3 2

CONTENTS

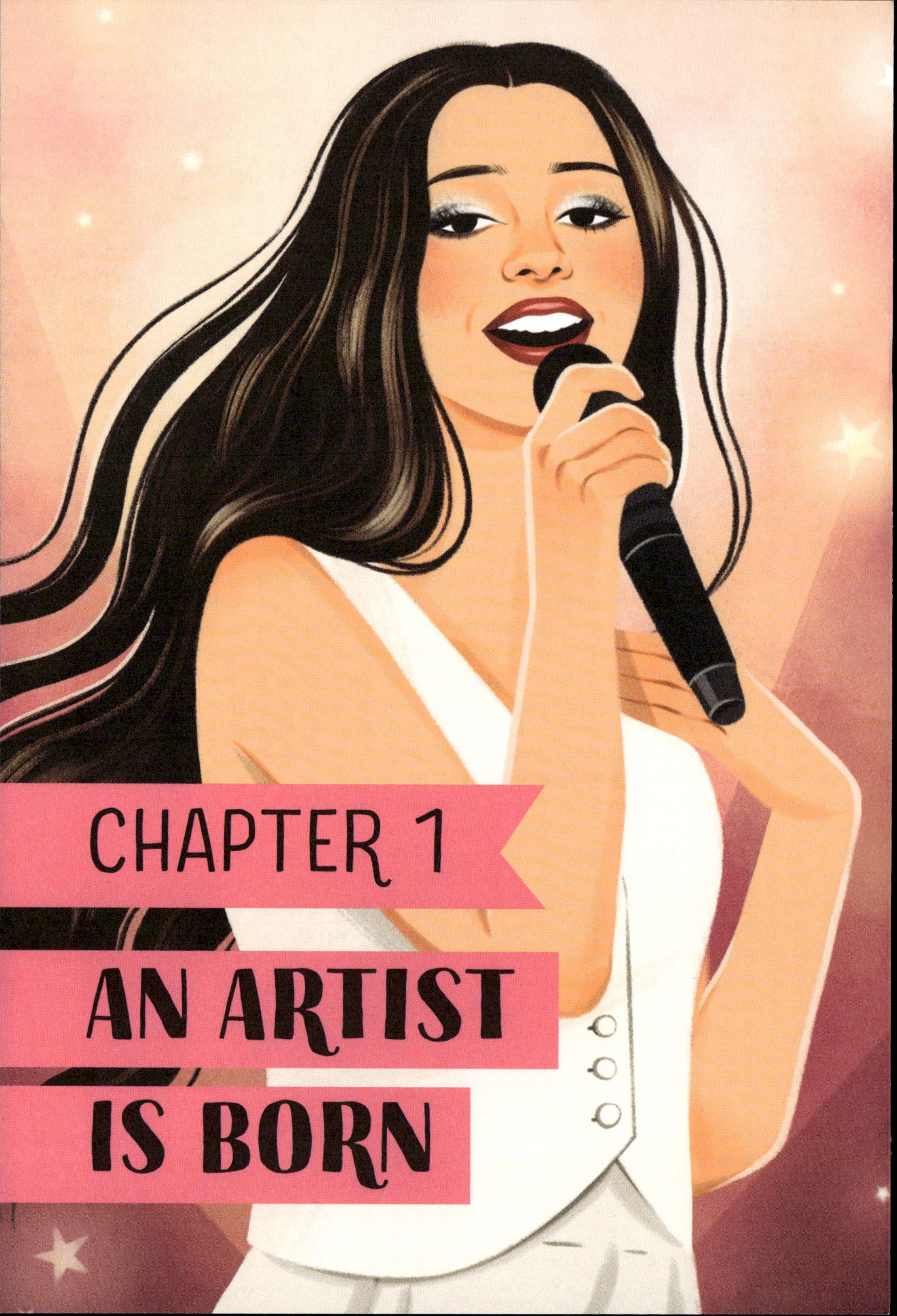

CHAPTER 1

AN ARTIST IS BORN

♪♩ Meet Olivia Rodrigo ♪♩

When Olivia Rodrigo was five years old, she knew that she wanted to be on stage. Her parents bought her a toy set to build play bridges. She made a microphone stand instead. Singing was her dream. How could a girl living in Temecula, California, 90 miles away from Hollywood, become a star?

She needed her parents' help. She liked singing but didn't play any instruments. Her parents signed her up for piano lessons. At first, Olivia didn't like playing piano. She cried before every lesson, but she didn't quit. After a while, Olivia began to understand what made some songs better than other songs. She started to write her own music and sing her own songs.

Olivia wanted to take acting lessons. Her parents signed her up. On weekends, she asked

JUMP IN THE THINK TANK

When you were very young, what did you say when someone asked what you wanted to be when you grew up? Do you still want that?

them to drive her to Hollywood for television and movie **auditions**. They agreed.

Young Olivia didn't know that someday, she would star in a popular Disney Channel television show. By the time she was 20 years old, she was going to win multiple **Grammy** Awards for her music. She would **perform** in sold-out arenas.

When she was a kid, all Olivia knew was that she had a big dream. Her parents told her that she didn't *have* to work so hard. But Olivia didn't want to take it easy.

Hard work didn't scare her. She refused to give up her dream.

Olivia Rodrigo was going to be a superstar.

♪ Olivia's World ♪

Olivia was born on February 20, 2003. She grew up in Temecula, California. Temecula is a small town in Riverside County. Tourists go there on weekends for an old-fashioned western boardwalk and hot-air balloon rides. Olivia's mom, Jennifer, was a teacher. Her father, Chris, was a family **therapist**.

In Olivia's house, her parents listened to **punk** and **alternative** rock music on the stereo or on a record player. This kind of music was usually fast, short, and easy to remember, and it often had **political** themes. Her parents loved popular groups like Pearl Jam, Green Day, No Doubt, and Weezer. But they also liked classical music and folk songs. They introduced Olivia to all kinds of music.

While Olivia was singing around the house, a new **country** artist named Taylor Swift moved to Nashville. Women were taking more leadership roles in politics and big companies. By the time Olivia turned five, the iPhone came out, opening a new way to connect. The internet began to change the world.

Olivia was always surrounded by music, but her childhood was also defined by the children's shows that were on TV. This was the era of

Disney and Nickelodeon shows like *Lizzie McGuire*, *The Suite Life of Zack & Cody*, *Zoey 101*, and *Hannah Montana*. When *High School Musical* came out in 2006, Olivia didn't know that someday, she'd be an actor and singer in that famous **franchise**.

Olivia had a lot of role models in her life, and soon, she would become a role model for others.

> "Most 14-year-olds aren't in a room with adults being like, 'So, what's your brand?'"

WHEN?

2003	2003	2004	2006
Olivia Rodrigo is born.	Taylor Swift moves to Nashville.	Facebook is launched.	*High School Musical* first airs.

CHAPTER 2

THE EARLY YEARS

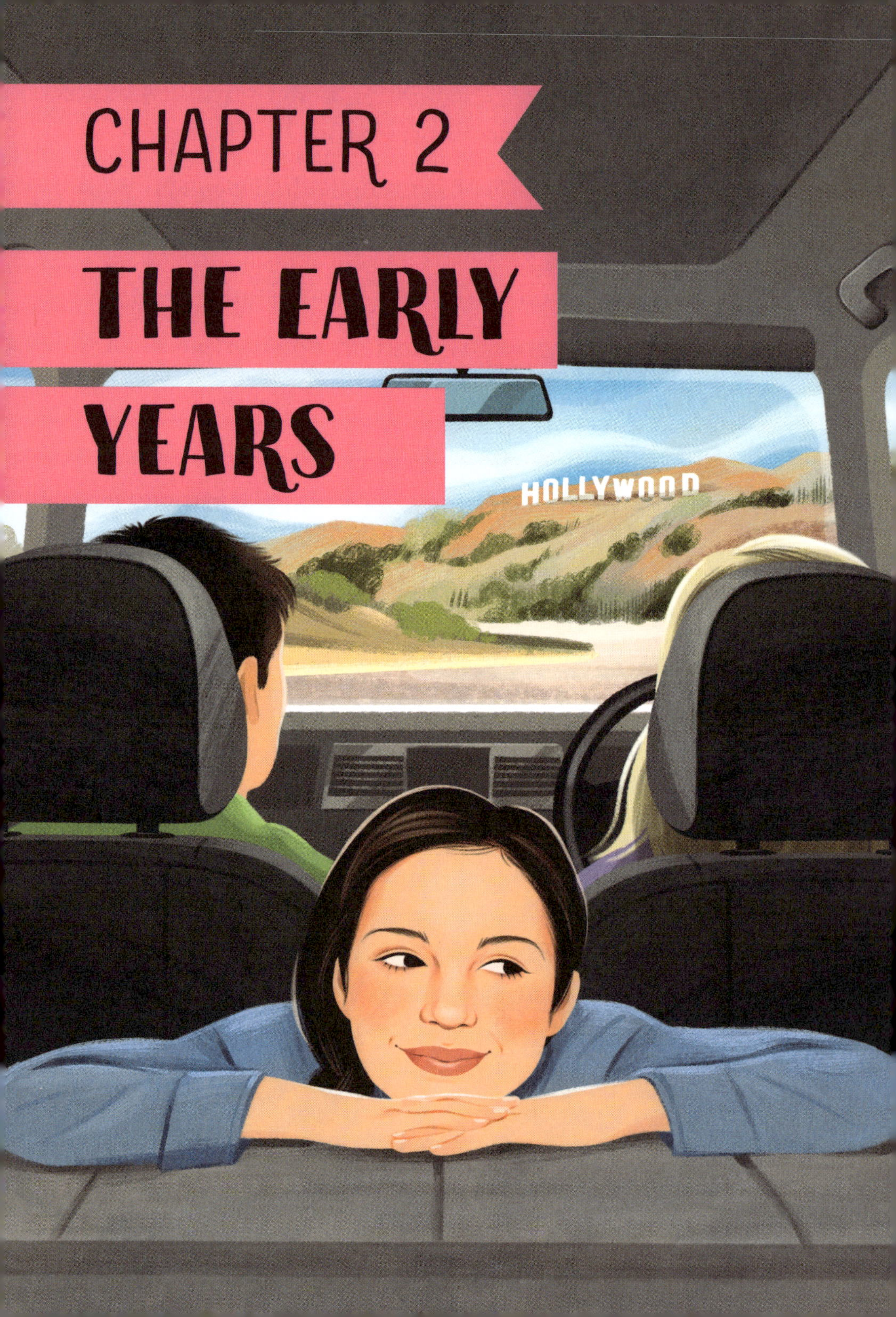

♪ Growing Up ♪

Olivia was influenced by both her parents' jobs. Her mom taught at a school, and Olivia always loved history and English. Her father was a therapist, and her parents taught her that emotions were important. Olivia was never afraid to scream or laugh or cry.

Family history was also important to Olivia. Her great-grandfather came to the United States as a teenager from the Philippines. Olivia didn't think very much about what it meant to be **Filipina** growing up because she was surrounded by people from all around the world. Once she was in Hollywood though, she realized that she represented something very special. Filipino Americans were some of her first fans. They celebrated her **career**. She wondered what it would feel like to travel all by herself to a new country, like her great-grandfather.

Olivia liked asking herself questions about how things *feel*. She said that her mom used to scream and dance to music. Olivia learned that music was supposed to bring on big feelings. Acting was also about feelings. When Olivia played a character, she imagined what that person felt like.

When Olivia was seven, she finally got an acting job! It was in an Old Navy **commercial**. She didn't have a big part, but she loved playing a shopper's daughter.

After that, Olivia auditioned for a lot of television shows and movies. All she heard was "No." Olivia and her parents would drive 90 miles to Los Angeles for auditions, then turn around and drive back home again. The ride would take two hours without traffic. If there was traffic, it could take four or five hours to get home.

JUMP —IN THE— THINK TANK

Do you know where your grandparents are from? What are some traditions you keep with them?

> "You can be super talented, **but if you don't show up,** what's the point?"

♪♩ Important Lessons ♪♩

When Olivia was nine years old, she told her mom she planned to be an Olympic gymnast. Her hero was Gabby Douglas, who was the 2012 all-around champion. That means she won in vault, bars, beam, and floor. Since Olivia couldn't do a decent cartwheel, she decided to stick to the dream she'd had since she was five instead: singing and acting.

Olivia had one big challenge to her dreams. Since she was a baby, she had partial hearing

MYTH	&	FACT
Olivia Rodrigo grew up in a quiet family.		Olivia's parents played loud music and loved to dance.

loss in her left ear. She didn't discover it until they did a hearing test in kindergarten. Headphones and hearing buds help people with hearing loss stay focused.

Year after year, Olivia worked hard and continued to audition. Her mom said that sometimes it felt like Olivia would do 50 interviews to get one really small role.

In Temecula, she continued to take acting lessons. She performed in school shows and small plays. She continued to play the piano, too. In her free time, Olivia would go to singing **competitions**. She sang songs that were popular.

Taylor Swift was on the radio then. Olivia decided that she'd like to be a **songwriter**, like Taylor. Perhaps songwriting was another way to reach her dreams?

Before Olivia turned 12, her parents told her they were tired of making the long drive to and from Los Angeles for auditions. Olivia wasn't getting jobs singing or acting. They told Olivia that if she didn't have a job by Christmas, it was time for her to find something else to do.

WHEN?

2006	2007	2008	2010
Taylor Swift releases her first album.	*High School Musical* 2 airs.	*High School Musical* 3 debuts.	Olivia appears in an Old Navy commercial.

CHAPTER 3

NEW ROLES

♪ Just in Time ♪

Olivia was worried. If she didn't find a job in Hollywood soon, her parents would stop taking her to auditions.

Finally, just before their Christmas deadline, Olivia was **cast** in her first movie. *Grace Stirs Up Success* was a film for American Girl. In the film, nine-year-old Grace Thomas visits Paris with her mom. While there, she learns to bake. After she returns home, she learns that her grandparents need money to save their business. She decides to take her new skills and audition for a baking contest. Grace wins the contest, helps her grandparents, and saves the day.

Grace Stirs Up Success also stirred up success for Olivia. Her performance got noticed by the people at the Disney Channel. They were casting a new show called *Bizaardvark*. Not only did Olivia get the job, but at the audition, she met her best friend, Madison Hu.

At their first meeting, the makers of the show wanted to see how they acted together. Everyone was surprised Olivia and Madison hadn't known each other forever! The truth was they had just met that day. From then on, they spent all their free time together.

Now that Olivia was going to be in *Bizaardvark,* her family had a big decision to make. They decided to sell their house in Temecula and move to an apartment

JUMP –IN THE– THINK TANK

If you had a choice, would you rather be a TV star, a movie star, or a singer?

in Los Angeles so they could be closer to Hollywood. It was time to focus on helping Olivia make her dreams come true.

♪ Life in LA ♪

Bizaardvark was the story of two best friends who have a video blog. Madison's character played the keyboard and piano. Olivia's character played guitar. The problem was Olivia didn't play guitar at the time. She started lessons. Her music teacher in Temecula said that Olivia was always most interested in the classes about being a singer and songwriter. She learned quickly. Soon, she was able to sing and play both instruments.

When the show was filming, Olivia's days were too busy to go to school. She was **homeschooled** instead. She didn't have very much free time. But when she did, she spent every moment with Madison. The two were always together off-screen. They traveled together, made **social media** posts, and had season passes to an amusement park. They both loved roller coasters. Olivia called Madison her soulmate and her best friend in the whole world.

When the show ended, Olivia's parents said she didn't have to keep acting if she didn't want to. But Olivia didn't want to quit. In fact, she wanted to do more: She wanted to sing, too.

The chance to do both came in 2019. *High School Musical* was a hugely popular movie

series. Now, Disney wanted to do a TV show based on the films. *High School Musical: The Musical: The Series* (*HSMTMTS*) needed actors who could sing and dance. At her first audition, Olivia and costar Josh Bassett sang together to see what they would sound like. Olivia said that the moment was magical. After that song, she was asked to play Nina "Nini" Salazar-Roberts on the show.

> "Learning to accept your quirks [is] part of life."

WHEN?

2015	2016	2016	2019
Olivia acts in her first movie.	The Rodrigo family moves to Los Angeles.	Olivia stars in *Bizaardvark*.	*High School Musical: The Musical: The Series* airs on TV.

CHAPTER 4

MAKING MUSIC

♪♩ The First Song ♪♩

Olivia's character on *HSMTMTS* was a songwriter. In the show, Nini had writer's block and struggled to create music. Olivia was asked to write a song for Nini to sing. Olivia wrote a song called "All I Want." She sang it as Nini on the fourth episode of Season One. "All I Want" was a **pop ballad** about relationships. The song debuted on a list of the most popular songs called the **Billboard Hot 100 charts** in January 2020. It became a Gold Record, which meant there were more than 500,000 **downloads**.

"All I Want" was a TikTok favorite. Now, Olivia officially knew she was talented at writing music. She wanted to write more songs! In her heart, she knew that she had to be careful. Disney's record company wanted her music for their **record label**.

She thought about it. A lot. Disney's record company liked to do things their own way.

Was it the right way for Olivia? She wanted to write songs about big feelings. In the end, she didn't think Disney was a good fit for her kind of music.

While filming *HSMTMTS*, Olivia wrote another new song called "Happier." It was about a girl who hopes her ex-boyfriend is not happy with his new girlfriend. She recorded it by herself and put it online. Once the song was on the internet, Olivia regretted posting it.

MYTH & FACT

MYTH: Olivia loved the version of "Happier" that she posted on Instagram.

FACT: She thought the video was embarrassing and considered taking it down.

She worried it was terrible, but she also knew it had the **potential** to be better.

Olivia needed help. But who could she turn to?

♪ Big Decisions ♪

It was important to Olivia to make the right decisions about her first **album**. "All I Want" caught the attention of two record companies: Geffen Records and Interscope Records. She went to talk to them. The people at Geffen agreed that Olivia could make decisions about her **recordings** and do things her own way. This was exactly what she wanted.

Olivia also knew she didn't want to make an EP. An EP is short for **Extended Play**. It's a short album with only four to six songs. A full album is known as an LP, which stands for **Long Play**. An LP can be seven to 29 songs. Olivia didn't want to be limited in the number of songs she could write. She asked Geffen if they would let her record an LP. They said yes.

JUMP -IN THE- THINK TANK

Olivia made big decisions. Who helps you make choices? Do you ask your friends or your family or just decide for yourself?

Olivia also asked for professional help from someone who knew how to make an album. She had never worked on a project like this before. The team at Geffen had a suggestion. They told her to call a **music producer** named Dan Nigro.

Olivia emailed Dan and sent him some samples of her music. He checked her out on Instagram. There, he discovered "Happier." Dan loved Olivia's style and messaged her with ideas of how they could work together.

Dan said that he could make her songs better. He would help Olivia make an album. This was *exactly* what Olivia wanted. She and Dan quickly became partners and friends.

Olivia officially signed a **record contract** with Geffen. She was ready to record her first album.

WHEN?

Olivia writes "All I Want."	2020
"All I Want" becomes a Gold Record.	2020
Olivia posts "Happier" to Instagram.	2020
Olivia meets Dan Nigro.	2020
Olivia signs with Geffen Records.	2020

CHAPTER 5

A RISING STAR

♪♩ Olivia the Songwriter ♪♩

As Olivia prepared to record her album, a **pandemic** suddenly forced everything to stop. COVID-19 is a virus that made people sick all over the world in 2020. People were told to stay home when they could and wear masks when they went outside. Olivia had to put her new album on hold.

That same year, the filming of Season Two of *HSMTMTS* was delayed for six months. During that time, Olivia wrote new songs. She had an idea for an album called *SOUR*. Olivia wanted to write every song herself. She knew Dan could help her make each song perfect when they were able to record again.

Olivia wanted to show emotions in her music. When Olivia felt sad, she wrote sad songs. When she felt happy, she wrote upbeat songs. Her emotions would make her music **relatable**.

JUMP —IN THE— THINK TANK

If you wanted to write a song, would you start with the tune, the beat, or the words?

Everyone knows what it feels like to be sad, happy, or lonely.

Olivia didn't let herself worry about whether her songs would be hits. She just wanted to tell her own personal stories. To do that, she studied poets and their **poetry**. Olivia wanted to see how other writers told their stories so she could tell hers. Olivia worked on the

words first, then added the music. She carried around a notebook to write down her thoughts.

Olivia felt that being alone when she worked on her songs was good for her. It allowed her to focus on her emotions and write songs from her heart. But now she was ready to start recording.

♪♩ Getting *SOUR* ♪♩

Because of the pandemic, Olivia stayed home in Los Angeles. She didn't have a fancy way to record her songs, so she did her best with her phone, her computer, and her own musical instruments. When she had a song ready, she would send it to Dan. He would make it better at his own **studio**, where he had recording equipment. Then they would email the song back and forth.

Once they were allowed to meet in person, Olivia and Dan went into a studio to continue working on new songs. By the time *HSMTMTS* was ready to film again, Olivia had her first song ready to release. Olivia shared "drivers license" online in 2020. People loved it. The song "drivers license" was one of the most successful songs of 2021 and made Olivia a superstar.

On April 1, 2021, Olivia released another song. It was called "deja vu." It reached Number 3 on the Billboard Hot 100 chart. Then Olivia let everyone hear "good 4 u." That song had over 1.6 billion **streams**.

A week later, the whole album came out. It was called *SOUR*. For Olivia, the word "sour" meant difficult feelings like jealousy and anger. She wanted everyone to know that those feelings are normal.

SOUR won two important music awards called Grammys: one for Best Pop Vocal Album and one for best Pop Solo Performance. Olivia also won the award for Best New Artist.

That summer, she went on **tour** and performed in 40 different cities around the world! Olivia was suddenly famous. While she was excited, she was also worried.

Fans were watching her, and they wanted to know everything: Who was she hanging out with? Where was she going for dinner? And when would she write more songs? Suddenly, she felt a lot of pressure to make another great album.

> "We're all feeling so much of the same things that we just don't talk about."

WHEN?

2021	2022	2022
Olivia releases *SOUR*.	Olivia wins three Grammy Awards.	Olivia goes on tour for *SOUR*.

CHAPTER 6

SHOWING GUTS

♪ Doing Good ♪

The success of *SOUR* gave Olivia a lot of attention. She decided to use her fame to tell people about issues that were important to her.

In 2021, she visited the White House and met President Joe Biden. She also talked to his medical adviser, Anthony Fauci. The three of them worked together to make videos about COVID-19 **vaccines**.

Olivia began to use videos and social media to raise money for **charities**. She designed T-shirts for a charity that helps young girls get an education. She gave some of the money she made on tour to another charity for women. Olivia made it her mission to help women with education, health, and safety.

Olivia was working so hard after *SOUR* that she needed a short break. She took time off to move into a new apartment in New York City.

She wanted to be close to her best friend Madison, who lived there. Olivia, Madison, and their friend Iris Apatow traveled, went to **concerts**, and posted a lot of photos on social media.

Olivia loved being with her friends, but it was also important to her to spend time alone so she could work on her next album. She wanted to make music that would push people to think about the world. The U.S. Supreme Court had just made a ruling that changed access to health care for girls and women. She was upset and wrote about it. Olivia also wrote about her feelings, breakups, friendships, and fame.

MYTH	&	FACT
Musicians have to live in Los Angeles, CA.		Musicians can live anywhere. Olivia moved to New York and got her own place.

Thinking about strength and power, she called her new album *GUTS*.

♪ A New Album ♪

Olivia wanted *GUTS* to have more fun and playful songs than *SOUR*. She felt happier in her life and decided to show that in her music.

She would still sing about feelings and politics, but the music would also show how much she'd grown up.

In June 2023, Olivia released her first song from *GUTS*. It was called "vampire" and it was a hit. Fans loved that she'd written another emotional song. It was the perfect song to come after the success of *SOUR*. Olivia was relieved. She had done it again!

Olivia's next two songs for *GUTS* were called "bad idea right?" and "get him back!" They were immediately popular, too.

Once the whole album was released, Olivia began to plan another world tour. On her *SOUR* tour, she had played in small theaters. On her *GUTS* tour, she would play in big arenas for the first time, sometimes to more than 20,000 fans. She planned to visit more than 77 cities around the world.

JUMP —IN THE— THINK TANK

If you wrote a song about your own feelings, what would it be called?

Olivia needed to prepare. She trained her voice and exercised. She rehearsed with her band. She worked with designers on the stage. And she learned complicated dance steps. Olivia remembered that on the *SOUR* tour, she was sometimes so tired that she slept for 14 hours. For the *GUTS* tour, she

made sure she would have time to sleep and eat healthy foods.

Olivia wanted to do one more thing before the tour began. She started her own charity, Fund 4 Good. It would raise money to help girls and women access health care, education, and more. Part of the ticket sales for each show on her tour would go to this charity. Olivia felt it was important to **inspire** girls to have strength when it comes to their own health and other important decisions.

WHEN?

Olivia moves to New York.
2023

Olivia releases the *GUTS* album.
2023

Olivia starts Fund 4 Good.
2023

CHAPTER 7

A BRIGHT FUTURE

♪ Star Power ♪

The *GUTS* album was nominated for six Grammy Awards, including one for Album of the Year. But at the awards show, Olivia didn't win any awards. Her fans were angry. They thought she should have won.

Olivia was too busy to get upset about the Grammys. She was having fun. Her album was a hit with her fans. The *GUTS* tour was a huge success. Olivia performed more than 80 shows around the world. Some of the countries she visited include Ireland, Spain, Japan, and the Philippines.

In 2024, Olivia appeared at a concert in Palm Desert, California. The band No Doubt was playing. They had been one of Olivia's favorites since she had listened to their music with her parents when she was little. The lead singer, Gwen Stefani, invited Olivia to perform with the band. Gwen introduced Olivia as "my little vampire," a nod to Olivia's own song. This was a huge moment for Olivia and one she would never forget.

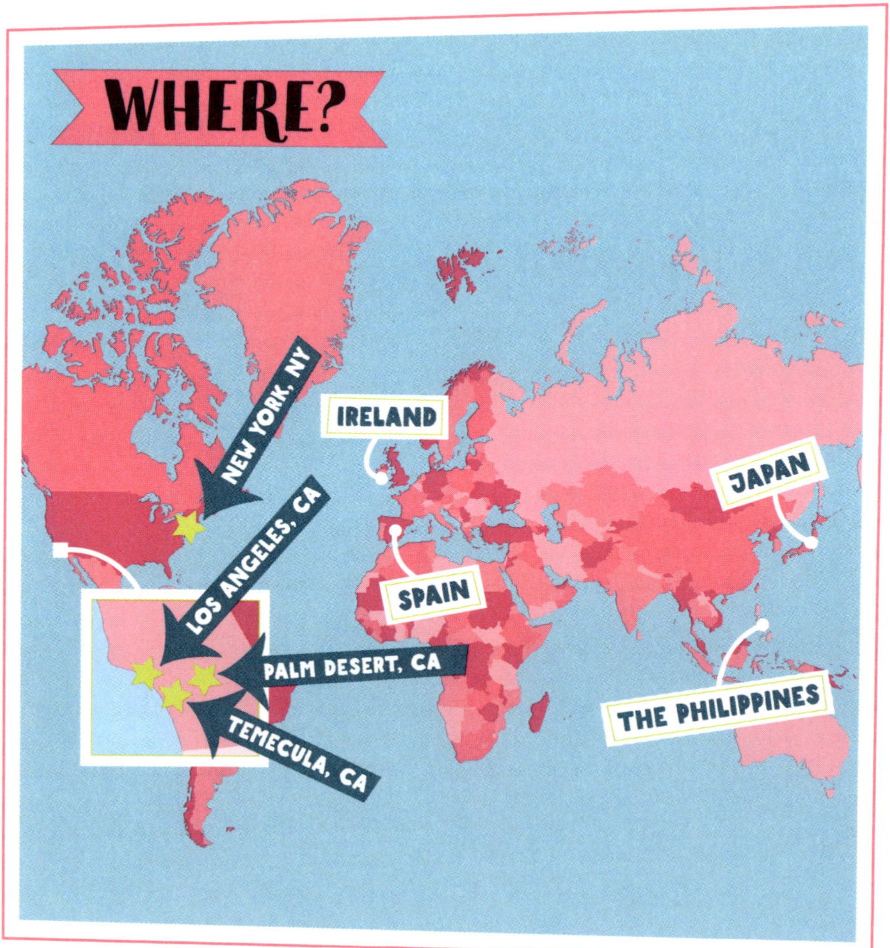

Olivia was also asked to write a song for a movie she was excited about. "Can't Catch Me Now" was featured in *The Hunger Games: The Ballad of Songbirds & Snakes*. Olivia was a big fan of the books that the movie was based on.

A lot of companies wanted Olivia to help **promote** their products. She became the face of a makeup line called Glossier. Crumbl Cookies even made a *GUTS* cookie! Olivia makes sure that all the products she works with are committed to helping the environment and donating to charities that she believes in.

JUMP -IN THE- THINK TANK

If you were going on a world tour, what are some places you'd like to visit? Where would you go first?

♪ Olivia's Legacy ♪

Olivia likes to share the details of her life with her fans. Through her music, she shares her emotions, from fear to sadness to joy. Her fans like that they can relate to Olivia because they feel the same things. Her messages are important to people all over the world.

Even when she was a kid, Olivia knew that emotions were important. Her parents taught her to always share what she was feeling. She remembered that as she became an actress, appearing in commercials, a movie, and then two television shows. Acting is all about showing emotions.

After Olivia starred on television, she learned to talk to her fans. From a young age, she grew up on screens and in front of crowds. Everyone was watching. Olivia dreamed of being a star and never quit. Now, being a star is her reality.

Olivia is focused on writing and performing music that connects with her fans. She gives money to important charities for women's health and speaks her mind freely. Olivia is a role model for young women, showing how to use their own power and strength to get what they need and to help others.

Olivia was asked about her life and what it feels like to be a big star. She said, "I've realized that I'm really not that special." She was saying what she always says: Her life is like everyone else's. This is what her fans love about her.

Whenever Olivia decides to make new music, her fans will be there, ready to listen.

> "I never want to stop learning and growing as a person."

WHEN?

2024 — *GUTS* is nominated for six Grammy Awards.

2024 — The *GUTS* world tour begins.

2024 — Olivia performs with Gwen Stefani.

2024 — The *GUTS World Tour* concert film is released.

CHAPTER 8

SO . . . WHO IS OLIVIA RODRIGO ?

♪♩ Challenge Accepted! ♪♩

Now that you know so much about Olivia's inspiring life and success, let's test your knowledge in this who, what, when, where, why, and how quiz. Feel free to look back in the text to find the answers if you need to, but try to remember first!

1 Where did Olivia Rodrigo grow up?

→ A Los Angeles, California
→ B Salt Lake City, Utah
→ C New York City, New York
→ D Temecula, California

2 What did Olivia want to be when she grew up?

→ A Singer
→ B Gymnast
→ C Therapist
→ D Teacher

3 **What was Olivia's first professional acting job?**

- A Target commercial
- B Old Navy commercial
- C American Girl movie
- D Broadway play

4 **What was the first movie Olivia starred in?**

- A *Grace Stirs Up Success*
- B *The Hunger Games*
- C *Star Wars*
- D *The LEGO Movie*

5 **When Olivia finally got an acting job on TV, where did her family move to?**

- A Los Angeles, California
- B Houston, Texas
- C Kansas City, Missouri
- D New York City, New York

6 **What was the name of Olivia's character in *High School Musical: The Musical: The Series*?**

- A Jessie
- B Wanda
- C Nini
- D Nancy

7 **What was the name of Olivia's first album?**

- A *BITTER*
- B *SOUR*
- C *TASTY*
- D *YUMMY*

8 **What was the name of the first song Olivia released from her first album?**

- A "good 4 u"
- B "drivers license"
- C "run away fast"
- D "vampire"

9 What movie did Olivia write a song for?

- A *Spirited*
- B *Marry Me*
- C *The Hunger Games: The Ballad of Songbirds & Snakes*
- D *Spider-Man: No Way Home*

10 What was Olivia's second hit album called?

- A *HEART*
- B *BRAVE*
- C *GUTS*
- D *BOLD*

Answer Key: 1. D; 2. B; 3. B; 4. A; 5. A; 6. C; 7. B; 8. B; 9. C; 10. C

♪ Our World ♪

Olivia Rodrigo shows the world who she is through her music and speaks up for what she believes in. Let's think a little more about what Olivia has done and how her success has affected the world we live in.

→ Olivia is a role model because she shares her feelings through her music. She writes songs when she is happy, sad, or even angry. These are feelings that everyone shares. She shows her fans that deep down, we are all the same.

→ Olivia is very honest about what she believes and never tries to pretend she's someone else. She donates her time and money to important causes. She wants the world to be better for young women, so she talks about meaningful issues. It takes bravery to speak out.

→ No matter how hard it was to be an actor or singer, Olivia never gave up. She worked toward her dream every day. If she didn't get a job at an audition, she went home and practiced more. Then, she tried again. She kept going until she got what she wanted.

JUMP IN THE THINK TANK FOR MORE!

Think about Olivia Rodrigo and answer these questions to keep exploring.

→ Olivia Rodrigo always dreamed of being a pop star. She never gave up that dream. What do you want to be when you are older?

→ Being famous means that everyone is always watching what you do. Olivia posts facts about her life on social media. Would you like being famous? Why or why not?

→ Olivia also gives a lot of her money to charities that help other people. What charities would you like to give money to? Who do you want to help?

♪♩ Glossary

album: a collection of songs

alternative: a type of music that doesn't follow traditional rules. It's about trying new sounds and lyrics.

auditions: tryouts where people do a short performance, like acting, dancing, or singing, to get a role in a movie or show

Billboard Hot 100 charts: rankings of the week's most popular songs and albums based on sales

brand: a person's public image and identity

career: the job a person has for a long period of time

cast: to choose actors or singers for a show or performance

charities: organizations that help people and support good causes

commercial: a short video that promotes a product or service

competitions: events where people try to win by doing something better than others

concert: a performance of music in front of an audience

country: a style of music that often tells stories about the lives of people in rural areas

downloads: content like music or videos that is downloaded, or transferred, from files on the internet to a device that can play it, like a smartphone or computer

Extended Play (EP): a short album with four to six songs

Filipina: a girl or woman from the Philippines, a country in Asia

franchise: a series of shows or products or businesses that are connected

Grammy: an award given to musicians for the best music each year

homeschooled: taught at home instead of in a school

inspire: to give someone the feeling or desire to do something

Long Play (LP): a full album, which can have seven to 29 songs

music producer: a person who helps musicians make their songs by guiding them and making decisions about the music

pandemic: an outbreak of disease that spreads around the world and makes many people sick in a short period of time

perform: to entertain an audience

poetry: a type of writing that uses words to express feelings and ideas in a creative way

political: related to the government or the public affairs of a country

pop ballad: a slow, emotional song that tells a story

potential: the ability to grow and become better at something

promote: to encourage people to like, buy, use, do, or support something

punk: a type of rock music that is often very loud and fast. It is all about being bold, different, and expressing feelings.

record contract: a written agreement between an artist and a record company

record label: a company that works with musicians to make and sell music

recordings: sounds or music that are saved, often in a digital file

relatable: when something is possible to understand because it feels similar to what you have experienced

social media: websites and other applications that enable users to create and share content

songwriter: a person who writes songs, creating both the music and the words

streams: instances when a song or video is played or watched online

studio: a place where audio recordings are made

therapist: a professional who helps others feel better by talking about their feelings

tour: a series of concerts by an artist or group of artists in different cities, countries, or locations

vaccines: medicines that teach bodies to fight off diseases and help keep them from getting sick

Bibliography

Anglin Stubbs, Jaharra. "Olivia Rodrigo's 'GUTS' Tour Spotlights Reproductive Justice Amidst Controversy." *Feminist Majority Foundation News*. March 20, 2024. Feminist.org/news/olivia-rodrigos-guts-tour-spotlights-reproductive-justice-amidst-controversy.

Biography.com Editors. "Olivia Rodrigo." Biography.com. Accessed November 8, 2024. Biography.com/musician/olivia-rodrigo#who-is-olivia-rodrigo.

Bruner, Raisa. "How Olivia Rodrigo Became America's Biggest New Pop Star." *Time*. May 24, 2021. Time.com/6050587/olivia-rodrigo-sour.

Carras, Christi. "A New Olivia Rodrigo Song Debuts Tomorrow. Here's an Exclusive Sneak Peek." *Los Angeles Times*. June 17, 2021. Latimes.com/entertainment-arts/tv/story/2021-06-17/olivia-rodrigo-new-song-high-school-musical-disney.

Houghton, Cillea. "Wise Beyond Her Years: The 10 Best Olivia Rodrigo Quotes." *American Songwriter*. Last modified August 15, 2023. Americansongwriter.com/wise-beyond-her-years-the-10-best-olivia-rodrigo-quotes.

Martoccio, Angie. "Olivia Rodrigo Is So Over Heartbreak." *Rolling Stone*. September 12, 2023. Web.archive.org/web/20230917060328/https://www.rollingstone.com/music/music-features/olivia-rodrigo-guts-vampire-lyrics-meaning-1234819181.

Shafer, Ellise. "From Disney to 'Drivers License': Inside Olivia Rodrigo's Musical Journey to Become the Voice of Her Generation." *Variety: 2021 Power of Young Hollywood Issue*. August 11, 2021. Variety.com/2021/music/news/olivia-rodrigo-drivers-license-sour-high-school-musical-1235038112.

Tolentino, Jia. "A New Decade, A New Album, A New Life—Olivia Rodrigo's Next Chapter." *Vogue*. July 6, 2023. Vogue.com/article/olivia-rodrigo-august-cover-2023-interview.

About the Author

STACIA DEUTSCH is a *New York Times* best selling author who has written more than three hundred children's books. She started her career with the award-winning chapter book series, Blast to the Past. Now, her résumé includes biographies of Amelia Earhart and Jim Henson in addition to junior movie tie-in novels for summer blockbuster films like *Boss Baby 2*, *Batman*, and *The Smurfs*. Her books include the popular *Girls Who Code: The Friendship Code*. New novels include a middle-grade series called Horse Club and a few stories for LEGO Ninjago. Stacia lives in Temecula on a small ranch with horses, dogs, and way too many wild bunnies. Find her at staciadeutsch.com, on Instagram @staciadeutsch_writes, and at facebook/staciadeutsch.

About the Illustrator

MARÍA PERERA was born in Gijón, a small seaside town in northern Spain. When she was very young, she found out that there were few things in life that she enjoyed as much as listening to The Beatles and drawing. She graduated in art history and soon after that she studied graphic design. She has worked as a freelance illustrator for several international publishers and magazines, and loves to work on portraits and children's books. She is very inspired by sixties and seventies music, literature, and cinema and loves to spend time with her family and friends. She still listens to The Beatles and feels fortunate to be able to do what she loves the most for a living: illustration.

WHO WILL INSPIRE YOU NEXT?

EXPLORE A WORLD OF HEROES AND ROLE MODELS IN ***THE STORY OF*** ...AN INSPIRING BIOGRAPHY SERIES FOR YOUNG READERS.

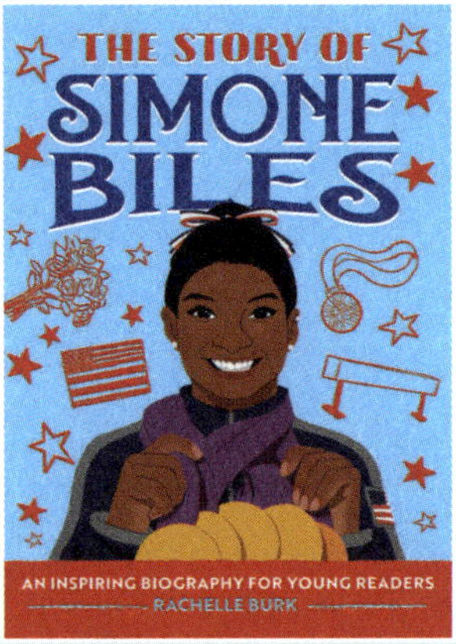

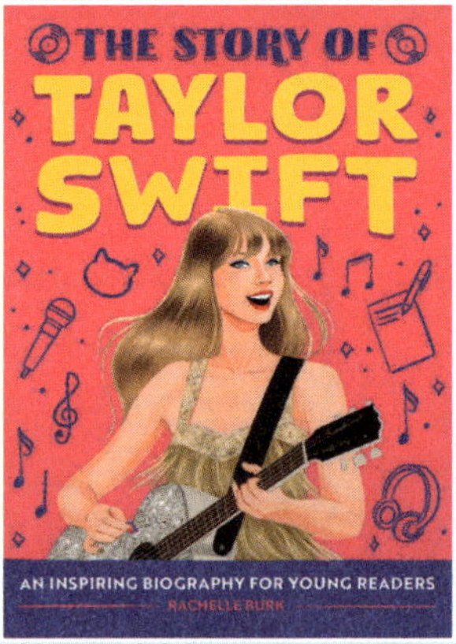

LOOK FOR THIS SERIES

WHEREVER BOOKS AND EBOOKS ARE SOLD